AUTISM AND
ANDROIDS

AUTISM AND ANDROIDS

PARIS TOSEN

Tosen Books

This is a book of nonfiction.

Copyright © 2013 by Paris Tosen

Book design by Paris Tosen

ISBN 978-1-926949-10-9

www.tosen.ca

CONTENTS

Preface 1

Reality scientist Paris Tosen looks at autism (ASD) from a technological viewpoint. As technologically ordained children, tens of millions around the world, they are not necessarily diseased and developmentally disordered, as what might appear to be. Are we witnessing the emergence of an advanced culture? The speaker has no medical training. This is his opinion based on his recent years of research into reality and synthetic life forms.

Preface

The discussion on autism and androids is a fundamentally new discussion, in my view, since I have not accumulated it from any academic or medical source, and I am not an expert in autism spectrum disorder (ASD). It comes about from the last 8 years of my life of intense study into the make-up of reality, the validity of our life form and the lost connection to the greater cosmos from which we are intimately derived.

So it is a rather profound discussion with immense implications as determined by an unscientific person. That said, there are some amazing aspects of autism that make a man like me a rather powerful resource for both the cause and cure of autism has eluded the great doctors and scientists for the past 70 years. No doctor has ever been able to cure autism and the reason why is because they have perceived it through a biological lens.

Why do I even care about children with autism? Because I don't want to see them huddled into a corner, fed drugs that don't work and for them to grow up as *disabled* people. And the reason is simple: these children are more advanced than you or me, they are more wonderful than you or me, and they have the right to be properly recognized as improved versions of ourselves. They are not developmentally disordered and socially inept.

Yes, it is true there are complications and there are corruptions in their systems, and some of them can be very severe and stressful for their parents and families. Still they deserve the proper recognition for what they truly are — advanced.

The reason I fell onto this subject stemmed from my discoveries of three androids on Capitol Hill as detailed in my book, *American Androids Critical Edition,* and a number of handmade YouTube documentaries on the subject. The androids I discovered, through observation and insight, looked human. For all intents and purposes they were human, but from my multidimensional observations, of these three individuals specifically, they were not. What bothered me was that no other scientist or conspiracy theorist had ever noticed what was plainly being broadcast on prime time US television.

This was Capitol Hill after all and these senior American politicians were media celebrities. They had been videotaped so many times that nearly all American citizens had seen them in one way or another over the many years of their collective careers. But in the fall of 2008, when George W. Bush & Friends rammed through a financial rescue bill that no one wanted, I happened to catch a white-haired Senator blinking like there was no tomorrow. He was the first and a powerful clue that we were not in Kansas, and never were in Kansas.

I had already determined the reality to be of some manufactured quality and having multiple dimensions, and I theorized that the human being was likely nonbiological. The reality research had me convinced but the nonbiological human was a bit more elusive. The political androids finally brought my theories to life. It led me all the way back to Jesus the Jewish messiah. More evidence, more theory. But the androids I could see on television. The anomalies I saw on three different individuals allowed me to see more androids in the populace. I did not detail these other discoveries because the synthetic characteristics were unconvincing to the general skeptic. Even people watched my videos and heard my in-depth discussions, still they could not come to the same conclusions. I had merely raised some very powerful questions regarding these characters. I was convinced and when I looked into society I was amazed at just how many synthetic cultures were among us.

So I am convinced that there are human-looking androids in society, in large numbers, and I can say this now after nearly 5 years of full-time study, which is good enough for a university degree somewhere. Some are innocuous and some are being controlled by a very advanced hidden hand, since after all robots are programmable people. This dark advanced race still eludes 99.99% of the world. A few people know of them. Most people have the wrong idea and look to the bible for clues. I looked to the television for the truth for it was plainly presenting itself and all that was required of me was to pay attention. I didn't need any prophecy or revelation to prove that it was the time of some apocalyptic event. But indeed 2008 was a biblical event that the bible and its scholars failed to scribble down.

Then I started paying closer attention to autism, from a generalized unscientific point of view. I utilized my new synthetic awareness to understand what was going on. I mean 1 in 88 children are diagnosed with ASD. That is a very significant disease, but what if it wasn't a disease? With my synthetic vision I never saw a disease; instead I saw a number of similarities to the other androids, properly functioning androids (for the most part). But what was amazing about autism in general was that these children were markedly different.

It was like they were being introduced to the world as completely new models but there was no one who was capable of understanding them. It was like introducing a product to the market too early and having no one to see the value in the invention. Over these several years, I watched with interest if autistic children would get some proper recognition for what they were rather than to point fingers at vaccines causing autism and new drugs (that don't work) for autism. What kind of drug do you give a robot? Will it cure him or her of her artificiality?

This is a very intricate situation and there are many interests. You might be a mother, sister, doctor or pharmaceutical corporation with an interest in autism. You might have been labelled as autistic yourself. I cannot satisfy all these different requirements. This has to remain a more generalized application of my multidimensional interests. Like I said, I am not a doctor and I am not qualified in treating any medical condition. Neither am I a scientist in any conventional meaning. I refer to myself as a reality scientist since that is what I have been doing for nearly 8 years. Regardless, what I believe I have uncovered is an impressive set of new thinking on autism and a new way to approach this alleged incurable condition. I think it also impacts Asperger Syndrome since there are some behavioural similarities and I have also found some connections to an older mental illness, Schizophrenia.

Autism, Asperger and Schizophrenia, in descending order, these are all inconveniently linked to my android research. But because we are dealing with children we are ultimately dealing with the evolution of human beings, the new generation. This is another touchy subject. The presence of autism in children means that children are being born with an entirely different set of features and these features are remarkably distinct from previous human generations, and the rate of their appearance is increasing such that more and more children are being born with these autism characteristics. My inclination is toward an advanced evolutionary process and their advancement is connected to synthetic organisms. This is very profound and it will have a crossover in my manufactured reality studies. I don't think I could have properly put this book together without my strong background now in reality physics, as I understand it thus far.

I come from the perspective that there are a multitude of other more advanced races of people besides humans. I am certain of that. In being certain of that it is logical to conclude that those cultures have advanced sciences at their disposal. What the best mind in human science is doing today, well, to a million-year advanced culture, of which I have met, they are millions of times better at it. We have tablet computers, they have holographic computers; they have instantaneous computers forming out of air. Can I prove what they have? Yes and No. The birth of autistic children, I think, is measurable proof that something has adjusted human DNA, and if it wasn't human geneticists, then it was nonhuman geneticists because the bees and the cows didn't do it. And having met Stelan races and seen some of their technologies I can say with a fair amount of confidence that they were involved in our genetic engineering. That also means that for a race of beings with an unquantifiable level of science, it would not be irrational to think that they know how to create life, and being far older than the human race, it would not be unreasonable to think they invented life.

In 2010, J. Craig Venter, an American biologist, invented the first synthetic cell using four bottles of chemicals and a computer. Imagine what a million-year advanced race can do? But I don't even think you need a race millions of years ahead of us because I think that kind of race is creating stars and planetary bodies, but, say a race of people 1,000 years ahead of Mr. Venter and his Research Group. That would be enough to create a person from scratch by creatively assembling DNA sequences. At the very least, a race like that could enter human society, without notice, and rearrange some of our DNA while we were sleeping or while a baby was in embryo state. The result would be the emergence of a mixed bag of new cultural characteristics.

Now say that a race 3,000 years ahead of humanity stopped by and handpicked a few women to be genetically upgraded. What would the result of that scientific intervention be? Well, it could be an advanced kid. A kid so advanced, genetically-speaking, that he wouldn't function well in this sadistic, fear-laden, noise-polluted, and corrupt world. A kid that would be considered disordered and would likely be autistic because we like giving names to those things that don't belong.

As you can see there are several permeable yet invisible factors involved in shaping the evolution of the human species. It is hard to overcome all the skepticism regarding these extraneous elements of influence but we can rely on the measurable truth. By my calculations there are approximately 20 million autistic kids in the world and this number is growing. The occurrence of ASD is increasing as our perception of it grows. The doctors and scientists have no cure and do not know the exact cause of this ever-growing disorder. The autism drugs seem to have failed to work and the one or two autism-specific drugs have not cured anyone. It has been 70 years and we haven't any real answers from the professionals.

I hope that I can provide some further illumination. I don't know if I have solved anything because there are too many intersecting fields of knowledge and quite a bit of scientific myopia. I am certain of one thing: the autistic person is not a biological person as we understand biological life forms. In order to eventually stabilize autistics we will have to upgrade our scientific models to include artificiality. This is fundamental to my discussion and I think central to finding a cure. Think advanced artificiality.

I am writing this book because I do not think anyone else is ever going to write it and we can't wait another 70 years of blind experimentation. I will not stand waiting as more autism drugs enter the market and seriously diminish the beauty of these children. Children who I am certain are a new class of synthetic-human cultures and not developmentally-disordered mutants.

I have to write this book because I have to inform people that autistic people are a newly forming class of people, as I will discuss. And we need to not only protect their presence here on earth but also to recognize them for what they truly are. In doing so, we will find new and innovative, hopefully outside the box, solutions and ways of interacting with these wonderful kids. I think that the cure can only be found if we shift the root of our thinking to artificial life and put aside biology, for these are artificial human beings dressed in all their biological glory.

CHAPTER 1

SYNTHETIC RACES OF PEOPLE

One out of 88 children (born in 2000) is born with Autism Spectrum Disorder (ASD), a developmental disorder characterized by abnormal biology and brain chemistry. This is according to research from the Center for Disease Control (and Prevention). "Autism spectrum disorders (ASDs) are a group of developmental disabilities characterized by impairments in social interaction and communication and by restricted, repetitive, and stereotyped patterns of behavior. Symptoms typically are apparent before age 3 years," reported the CDC from a 2008 surveillance year. Most of the data comes from children aged 8 years, from all racial, ethnic and socioeconomic groups, and the trend has been increasing. In a

2000 surveillance, the prevalence of ASD was 1 in 150 (born in 1992). If the trend continues, we can expect many children born in 2013 with these developmental characteristics.

Children represent 25% of the human population; a figure derived from North American demographics (and carried over for the rest of the world). There are 7 billion people in the world. If 25% are children, as a rough estimate, then there are 1.75 billion children.

Given the ratio of ASD appearing in children of North America (1 in 88), and averaging out the variations that would appear in each region, there are (roughly) 20 million autistic children worldwide, according to current standards. These 20 million kids with ASD will form the basis of our discussion.

There are more autistic children in the world than there are people in Sweden (pop. 9.4 million). The population of Sweden, an entire nation, is smaller than the population of autistic children. Likewise, there are more ASD kids than the 11 million people in Greece and the 13 million people in State of Illinois. And just about the same amount of autistic kids in the world as people in Australia (pop. 23 million). Verily, on the surface, we could (easily) argue that the ASD child population is significant enough to be considered worthy of a national cultural status. But autism is not yet an independent culture; rather it is widely understood to be a neurological disorder peppered with behavioural and developmental regression, mental retardation, and cognitive impairment.

It is believed that autism affects the way the brain functions. The implications on the brain result in difficulties in social interaction and communication with people (withdrawn, prefers to be alone, lack of empathy, repeats words). There are also unusual patterns of behaviour, activities, movements (repetitive movements) and interests (strange attachments to everyday objects). The changes in behaviour are attributed to an unknown cause of an autistic spectrum. In other words, the medical community generally observes that the condition is *internal* to the patient. Some internal chemical or biological mechanism, genetic predisposition or environmental agent, results in a handicapped personality and persona that requires specialized education.

It is considered a spectrum disorder because of a continuum of severity from mild to severe; the age of onset is flexible; boys are more likely to be affected; family income, lifestyle, education do not affect risk of autism; and the types of challenges in social environment can vary. ASD is under PSD (Pervasive Developmental Disorder) as well as Asperger Syndrome and Schizophrenia. Despite all of these attributions and diagnoses some autistics are considered high functioning people. Some have gifts and high-tech abilities. Some cases are very severe.

The cause of ASD is unknown. According to Wikipedia, classic autism was first recognized in 1942 by Dr. Leo Kanner at John's Hopkins Hospital. Austrian psychologist, Hans Asperger, described a similar group of patients around the same time. The diagnosis of autism coincidentally occurred at nearly the same time that the three political androids were born, between 1940 and 1943. That puts both autism and androids at the time frame of WWII since the birth of the three android politicians was at exactly the same time as the emergence of autism. This in my view cannot be seen as a coincidence and having no predisposition or interest for autism, in other words my android research was unrelated to an autism research, it makes the relationship all that much more significant. It makes sense to see the birth of a pure synthetic subculture coincide with the birth children with synthetic genes.

The probable start of WWII was 1939 on 1 September. In the years prior to the invasion of Poland the Germans were heavily involved in forced sterilization and compulsory euthanasia for the mentally and physically unfit, a practice that originated from America's forced sterilization programs and which received funding from the Rockefeller Foundation. In three years in the mid-30s, 400,000 people deemed abnormal were sterilized and later 100,000 were gassed. The eugenics policies were later continued and used widely in the Jewish concentration and extermination camps. The idea was to purify the Germanic race (Nordics) and to improve the genetic composition of the population. These eugenics programs later evolved into developments in genetic, genomic and reproductive technologies.

The appearance of autism in the early 1940s coincides with the improvement in eugenics practices. Could it be possible that the purification of genes and the modifications on human genomes led to some cases of highly pure human beings? These exceptional cases would not have been accidental and could have been limited to a certain proportion of genetic displacement in order to prevent an imbalance in human population. An imbalance in the human gene pool would have led to an imbalance in human evolution.

Imagine if one nation had 100 more IQ points than any of the top nations. The brain power of that one nation would lead to world domination. On the other hand, the dispersion of purified genetic samples, people, across the global population would lead to a more stable allotment of cross cultural ideas and would prevent the elite domination of any particular race unless the notion of racial supremacy was maintained in a particular nation. The democratization of eugenics would be the only way to ensure a properly functioning world.

In the early parts of the 20th century, eugenics was promoted by the wealthy class and their institutions of preference. Even governments were involved in the reproduction of certain people and traits. The eugenics discussion today would likely result in forceful opposition and these practices at genetic engineering would be considered human rights violations. At the same time the organizations involved in genetics do not promote eugenics as their main practice; instead they've invented a new industry, *biotechnology*.

In the biotechnology business living organisms are modified according to human purpose. In agriculture, plant seeds are improved or hybridized to create genetically-modified crops. Medicines are tailor-made for specific genetic conditions or predispositions. Genes are tested for mutated sequences and people's personal genetic information is stored for some unknown future use. Some of these discoveries have led to gene therapy, the process of replacing a defective gene with a normal gene and even the controversial artificial vaccines. The latest commercial practice of biotechnology involves the synthesizing of a gene without a normal DNA sample.

These commercialized gene synthesis services can create stretches of DNA at market price. The latest development under J. Craig Venter, an American biologist who was the first to sequence the human genome, involves creating synthetic biological organisms. In 2010, Venter and his team successfully synthesized the genome of a bacteria from a computer record, in other words, the parent of the bacteria was a computer.

Essentially, the central theme of this book is a *computer-based life*. The best publicly available genetic practices has shown success with bacteria. The real catchphrase of this topic, surely, is "computer-based existence." There are some difficult presuppositions, as with all of my work, and this is because much of my understanding is based in cosmic science and cosmic science has no equivalent human science. Fringe science is perhaps several steps closer than the rest and quantum science is well on its way. Sadly, the closest similarities in modern day can be found in science fiction novels and movies.

But the extensive genetic investment in bacteria represents an entirely, even primarily, human-based endeavour. The discoveries in chromosome software and cellular identity are the very early state of an eventual existential science. This is the kind of science that can sustain life and involves many genes and many cells all interconnected into one symbiotic device, the human being. The invention of a synthetic cell by Craig Venter and his group, if multiplied by 1,000 years, leads to the creation of life, verily the creation of a species of *human beings*.

The simple synthetic cell multiplied by a million years leads to the creation of races of people, civilizations. This synthetic alchemy multiplied or evolved by a billion years, science that is a billion years ahead of the best human science, leads to the creation of planetary bodies and plasma-generating Suns. Unfortunately, our minds cannot think on those scales and, for the most people, we are appropriately distracted by celebrity, war and infectious outbreaks that require additional vaccine shots. But if we were to think on these scales, if we could look at science evolving one million years we could not logically resist or deny the fact that an entire race of people could be created.

Look at the genus of hominids and their slow evolution over millions of years. Modern humans originated in Africa about 125,000 to 200,000 years ago and reached maturity about 30,000 to 50,000 years ago. Prior to this genus of Homo there were quite a few other hominid types, basically primates. Even today humans are scientifically classified as mammals under the order of primatess. Human DNA is 95% identical to that of chimpanzee. In fact chimpanzees, and gorillas, are human relatives. We diverged from chimpanzees and gorillas several million years ago, but our roots are still primate-based.

The evolution of an intelligent species is accompanied by developmental change, physiological change and behavioural change. Our Human Line has a more developed brain (larger cranial capacity), better languaging skills, problem-solving abilities, abstract reasoning and even the power of introspection. Modern humans also have other thought processes like wisdom, the comprehension of truth coupled with correct judgment and action. Some humans have self-awareness and rationality. Fewer still have morality.

While cranial capacity hasn't changed, what indeed has changed is a remarkable internal intelligence. Much like the new computers of today, the microprocessor reached its structural limits so to increase the processing power of a computer they invented multi-core architectures. The appearance of an autistic Diaspora embedded with an amazing intelligence, awareness and sensitivity represents the appearance of a new genus of hominids. Remember that evolutionary trends included developmental, physiological and behavioural change and children with ASD certainly have many new characteristics on this level. The difference is that ASD kids have been diagnosed as *abnormal and impaired*, and this is something I do not agree with. Certainly there are severe cases of ASD, but from my observations the majority of children suffer only minor symptoms, and no more different than puberty. We don't diagnose and treat kids for going through puberty and that is because we understand that this is a developmental phase. What is ASD, and all its related acronyms, is also a phase, the kind of which we are not used to?

What if to increase sentience of a human at the genetic level, they created new faculties of cognition at some other subatomic level, perhaps a higher dimensional scale or frequency so that the autistic child has a kind of multi-core neurological hardware, or a multidimensional mental framework. A higher frame rate of perception leading to an increased acuity of the environment, all done through the attenuation of genes. A comparative scientific investigation into key sequences of genes would be an interesting research project.

The sheer significance of children considered to have ASD, Asperger and even (to a lesser extent) Schizophrenia (it is in fact an older condition) is not something to be taken lightly. In fact, I strongly feel that they represent the birth of a new genus of Homo: a species that is cosmically-ordained and has its root not in primates, but, rather in interstellar races, *Stelans*. The autistic children are a mix of Cosmic and Stelan genes. And cosmic is another term for *synthetic* because, as I have observed, the cosmos is not biological in any sense. It is a highly advanced and gargantuan synthetic architecture based in the software of DNA.

The Medieval Latin word, *celestialis*, pertains to the spiritual or invisible Heaven, even an *inhabitant* of Heaven. Autistic children are better identified, I think, as a *Homo celestialis*, a "heaven-made man". In Latin the term is "caelesti," meaning heaven + sky. If I were to give the autistic Diaspora a new name, I would call them *Caelans* for they are these highly advanced heaven-sky species, a split from the primates unlike ever before. We could modify the spelling for ease of use and simply call them *Kalans*. We would have Humans, Stelans and now *Kalans*, in my world order.

Kalans would represent a new genus of Homo with a *root* in Stelan genetics, as opposed to a Human root in Primate genetics, and having been interbred with Cosmic DNA, essentially synthetic genes with a cosmic signature. Those cosmic genes, since they are synthetic, needn't any specific parent. As Craig Venter and his Team proved not many months ago, the parent of a self-replicating organism can be a *computer*. What if one of the parents, perhaps the father of an autistic child was a computer, not your average desktop version, rather a highly advanced cosmic machine having no terrestrial comparison. The Kalan Culture would represent an entirely new earth-based culture having little or no primate DNA characteristics of any significance.

Again, I am not a geneticist nor am I an anthropologist, but I am aware of a historical upgrading of the human genome by various interstellar races. But you don't need to be a geneticist to make this observation, something that the scientific community will argue, you only need to look at the iPhone and the wireless internet. Our technological advancements can only be explained by radical shifts in our DNA. Just yesterday, we were living in caves and hunting for food. Today, we are downloading songs from the internet and have an international space station. The humans of the last 100 years are already a divergence from the previous *Homo sapiens* because humans of today have a significant amount of Stelan (interstellar) genes. In fact, we could say that anyone under 30 years old is probably mostly Stelan anyway, from a genetic level.

Kalans, on the other hand, are upgraded Stelans and are more cosmically-oriented; therefore they are more synthetic than interstellar, or any mix of the two. We would have to improve our study of gene sequences to truly figure out the new DNA combinations. Certainly, they haven't the primate root humans once had and I think, and scientific research will eventually disclose, they represent a new synthetic race of people. The kind of synthetic superiority (or improved species) unlike anything we have ever imagined. And that being the case, if my observations are correct on this matter, we could say that any organism derived from the cosmos, to one degree or another, is synthetically ordained, including the slowly fading Humans.

CHAPTER 2

NO MACHINE IS PERFECT

As the human genome evolves and further interacts with the artificial construct of reality, we will see the brain's relevance diminish. Most likely the brain will become a commodity organ that will not be as important as the internal architecture (eg energy body, DNA) of humans. We see this shift in the computer industry as microprocessors are scaled down further and further. Intel, a pioneer of the microprocessor, has invented transistors smaller than DNA and transistor-based cells smaller than a red blood cell. In more recent years, Intel has invented "high-k" materials to replace the silicon dioxide (SiO_2) used in transistors. Hafnium dioxide (HfO_2), for example, can hold more electric charge with less leakage and are suitable for use in nanoelectronic transistors that start in the 45nm (nanometre) node.

The molecular electronics discussion has been around for at least 30 years and atomic computers, using atoms as internal pathways, are not far around the corner. To think that a human being, made up of molecules and atoms, couldn't have been created by some other scientific tradition is idealistic. Given the immense technological leaps in the last 150 years, imagine what we could be doing in 40 years. Artificial beings are not out of the question. And now consider what an already in existence advanced race has already done— living beings.

When I uploaded my observations of the androids on Capitol Hill at the tail end of 2010, I immediately received a number of queries asking for a scientific explanation. With some incredible luck, I discovered that the rapid eye movements on two of the synthetic people were linked to a mid-brain structure called the *substantia nigra*. The substantia nigra, not a very well known structure, is rich in *melanin*, a black pigment. What was interesting of melanin was that it had organic polymer attributes and a powerful electroluminescent quality. By applying a voltage to melanin you could switch between states. I fringe concluded that the robots were being remote-controlled via the substantia nigra structure because the melanin was being used as a switch. The robot could be wirelessly turned on and controlled and then turned off. In off-mode, the robot would revert back to basic programming. In on-mode, the robot was under the control of some other unidentified user. In the early 1970s, researchers developed organic electronic devices, one of them was a *melanin switch*. Dr. John McGinness was one of the early pioneers of organic electronics, the kind of science that would take decades to truly appreciate.

Instead of creating a laptop computer, or automobile, we'd be creating synthetic people, *Kalans*, but these synthetic people look and act like real people. They appear to be completely biologically-based life forms. They are not biologically-based. We know that. They appear to be biological on the surface. On the surface our manufactured race of people are biological people. We'd know otherwise. If we didn't inform our synthetic race that they were synthetic and we reminded them that they are planetary beings based in biology then they wouldn't ever realize their synthetic origins. In fact, a synthetic person can never realize that they are synthetic. Why? Because that would violate a fundamental Law of Creation: you cannot share a level of knowledge or information that the recipient is incapable or unable to comprehend. As creators of this synthetic race, we could not violate our own laws of creation, or protocols of synthetic science. After all, we created these laws and protocols for good reason. But at some point in the evolution of our synthetic race of people we'd have to have them come to this understanding for it is a proper process of development, to understand one's origins.

As well, if there were reasons preventing this disclosure, for example, if some of our scientific team went rogue and decided to run the synthetic world they helped to create, they could artificially reduce or suppress their awareness interfaces and this would delay an awakening. This induced suppression would also prevent the moral scientists from sharing this knowledge because it would break their own laws of creation.

Sooner or later, as our synthetic race of people continue to develop and grow, as determined by their programming, their own synthetic cellular technologies and chromosomal software would gain increasing complexities and these complexities would also give rise to anomalous individuals or even groups. These anomalies would be like super computers because they would have embedded in them some advanced characteristics of a phenomenal quality. Of course, not all of this is random since as the creative team behind this desolated planetary body inhabited with artificial beings we'd still be around. We would never abandon any scientific experiment just as we wouldn't abandon our children, unless we were irresponsible. As creationary scientists, we are steeped in an impressive array of existential guidelines and codes of professional conduct.

The anomalous individual, for example, would be an exceptional specimen. They'd be famous or genius, perhaps even both. They they'd be on television. But there is an assumption to this anomalous model which needs some attention because wherever we deal with synthetic existence, as in any scientific enterprise, we are dealing with errors and corruption. Our creative combination would be done in error; this error could lead to a deformity, an additional arm, a warped skull, a penchant for chatter.

As well, the anomalous individual's genes might have been made susceptible to corrupt code and this synthetic virus, for whatever reason could have crippled or handicapped the individual. We see this in the computer world already. A powerful new computer could have a software bug that "cripples" or "handicaps" the computer. This can also be the case with some of our super beings.

They are so impressive technologically that there may be bugs that need to be worked out. Eventually, these bugs will be fixed with improvements in the operational software (aka DNA), but for now these people might appear to have abnormal qualifications, especially when compared to the norm. And because their genius is handicapped they won't have the notoriety of the stars and the famous example.

No machine is perfect all the time. The more advanced the machine, the more maintenance it requires. If the maintenance schedule is not maintained then the machine starts to malfunction. The chromosomal software starts to experience corrupt code. Our synthetic model runs into addictions and destructive behaviour. If noticed early enough these bugs and corrupt genetic sequences can be corrected and the individual could become a superstar, but if the defective code were left alone or the individual refused treatment then the individual could live the rest of their life on substandard terms. Their lives could be shortened.

The appearance and rise of an autistic class of people, as mostly children, is a good representation of the kinds of situations that any synthetic species experiences. It is generally regarded to be the introduction of new models or new versions. The difference between new models of people and new models of cars is that we generally love the latest model of car or phone, but when new models of people show up, and we're stuck on biology, we rely on primitive thinking to understand advanced existential bodies.

The autistic child, considered to have abnormal developmental conditions, is a perfect example of a super computer being introduced in a desktop computer market. These advanced children represent the latest genetic variants and have an impressive chromosomal array. By the same token they are being forced to live in a highly subdued world that is beset by a still primitive view on what is best in life. The autistic child is not abnormal, they are advanced. They are genetically superior to the main societal group, but rather than being interpreted as advanced models of people they are being labelled as handicapped.

If you were to take a new Ferrari and drive it on a dirt road full of hills and mud, the Ferrari would appear to be handicapped. The Ferrari is being forced to drive in off-road condition when it should by right be driven on a smooth asphalt highway.

The autistic child is like a Ferrari in a Toyota and GM marketplace. These children are not vehicles per se but as technological beings the automotive analogy is a good descriptive. We are experiencing a technological deviation in the normal population and this deviation is superior on every aspect. Some of these autistic tendencies and superior cellular codes may not be activated and will remain dormant according to present environmental conditions and their internal programming. So the autistic child may grow increasingly complex under the right conditions, but under poor conditions they might remain in a crippled or severely withdrawn state of existence.

The key is to realize that the fundamental condition of their birth and appearance is rooted in superior chromosomal software systems. They may have bugs and contaminated code but they are advanced people who belong to an advanced civilization. Rather than trying to normalize their skills and abilities so as to make them *appear* normal, it is better to have them expand on their advanced skills and learn to stabilize their bodies in the current environs because some autistic children can have violent or repetitive behaviours and they could be harmful. These conditions could be related to bugs or to cross interference in the environment. There are environmental factors in the manufactured reality that could inspire these harmful behaviours or addictions to objects or thoughts, everything in their highly sensitive

person can be magnified. Their systems of
perception are extremely advanced and coupled
with environmental interference or adverse
chemicals this would create chaos in their
advanced existential code.

There are many challenges to discussing this
kind of material most of which include
exceeding human standard logic and stepping
outside the bounds of human science, but the
challenge of understanding cannot mistake the
remarkable presence of unnaturally-gifted
people among us. My attribution to their
reconciliation is based in synthetic advancement
and that is because we live in a synthetically
based realm. Ultimately that kind of discussion
is another discussion itself. This book is on
autism and I think the presence of advanced
children only reinforces our need to protect
these new peoples from any primitive
interpretation or any ridiculous cure. There is no
cure for autism because there is no autistic

disorder or disease. **These are synthetically advanced human beings.**

The question remains as to whether they are still human since they are a very different breed of existence. The reason that there is no known cause for ASD is because science cannot think outside of its own regressive enterprise. The reasons for autism spectrum disorder include advanced genetic structure, remarkable DNA encoding, impressive chromosomal software and a fantastic connection to the cosmic internet. The reasons for them appearing disordered include outdated orthodox scientific models, a polluted environment, toxic chemicals in food, medications that distort sensitive existential systems, corruption and defects in genetic code, and an unwillingness to embrace them as the new humans. Verily, autistic children should be given a new cultural label, one that replaces "human" because, after all, these advanced people are here to replace the rest of us, as a natural process of evolution. Evolution is the process by which societies and species are upgraded at the genetic level. Indeed, these mislabelled autistics are advanced versions of human people.

CHAPTER 3

THE MAGICAL CHILD

The autistic child is a magical child when fully and properly understood as a person for their complexity is so impressive that they appear to be magical. The magical qualities of an autistic child have been misinterpreted as a child of disorder, disability and an indeterminable unusualness. As we explore the magical qualities of the autistic child and adult we discover a new unscientific view of this biological complexity. This unscientific view is wholly rooted in reality physics, a newly invented science to explain the multidimensional universe, the very same universe we all inhabit and in which we collectively partake.

The universal structure of existence is not rooted in biological life forms, rather the universe is manufactured by an immeasurable set of technological instruments and therefore the root of existence, at its most fundamental quotient from creation itself, is *nonbiological*. This nonbiological view of existence is an imperative compassion to understanding the magical qualities of the autistic person because the autistic person is qualitatively nonbiological; that is to say that an autistic child is a child that is in close harmony to the universe. And the universe is a manufactured set of technological constructs.

What do we mean when we use the term like nonbiological? Biology is fixated on the predictable patterns of molecular machines such as proteins, bacteria, mitochondria and DNA. These temporary machines are underneath the presence of life, a readily identified definition of biology, the study and science of life and living organisms. If biological refers to a living organism of natural quality then nonbiological refers to an organism that is alive by artificial means.

The trouble with artificiality is that the general conception of artificial rests in the hands of human inventors and humans are a very young species in the universe; therefore whenever a young species invents artificial devices those devices are less superior than their natural comparatives. For example, a human brain is still more powerful than a computer brain. The human brain is a natural device weighing only 3 pounds. The computer brain is an artificial machine and could weigh hundreds of pounds and still not be able to outmatch its human equivalent. Human invention has not been able to out-invent its own limitations unless aided by some extra-dimensional force or inspiration.

The rash of 20th century technologies—microprocessor, television, satellite, rockets, internet, mobile telephony, microwave ovens, fibre optics, social networks—are well outside the capacity of biological beings. In fact, the 20th century must necessarily be perceived as an anomalous period and an anomalous period such as the 20th century is a period in which human science and invention was aided. Any rational person must be able to see that the 20th century is an impressive technological explosion and it would appear, on the surface, as if humankind woke up, but what if this is not the case. What if humankind didn't only wake up but it was instrumentally influenced? It was influenced on such an instrumental level, from inside and out, that it was perceived to have improved itself.

Some pervasive questions remain: how can a purely biological, natural life form create an artificial, technological transistor radio or a cathode ray tube television? How can a genetic being invent a wireless internet? While we try very hard to avoid asking these kinds of questions or quickly found simple answers such as geniuses invented these technologies, we instinctively know better. There's no way for a purely biological creation to invent a purely nonbiological creation. The only way that is possible is if the biological creation is itself nonbiological. A chicken can lay an egg but a chicken cannot make chicken soup. A chicken cannot invent a wireless hand phone and neither should a human being. But clearly we are seeing mobile phones in use today so this technological capacity is clearly possible.

The only way to invent technology is to at first be technological yourself. No human can invent a technology unless they themselves are technological or at the very least have had technological assistance. A television can never form out of neurotransmitters unless those neurotransmitters were nonbiological. There must be included in the equation of technological innovation a level of symmetry.

Symmetry is woefully absent in human life. Human beings are happy to accept the credit for all of their inventions and are confident to bring out their biologically-based theories to explain everything. Human logic and reason have an answer for almost everything. I say almost because the things outside their scientific models of rationality fall into supernatural or spiritual dimensions. If there is no answer they all turn to God.

This then has been the basic human model for progress, evolution and development. On a fundamental level, this model has worked to allow the human race a chance to evolve. But there are some hiccups along this limited road for biology is a limited model; biology is a temporary (or mortal) justification for things to be. We notice our misunderstanding when we hit things we don't understand. I identified in *American Androids* one of our biological weaknesses when I discussed the mysterious outbreak of Encephalitis lethargica, a brain inflammation that started around 1916.

Encephalitis lethargica is an impressive disease brought on by some unidentified neurotoxin. The disease has no cause and no cure, but the outbreak was restricted to the time of World War I. In the early 1920s, the outbreak put many people to sleep and to death. Some of those fell into a deep sleep and wouldn't wake up for decades. By 1969, with the experimentation by Dr. Oliver Sacks, a synthetic dopamine (L-Dopa) would be introduced to a set of patients and these patients would miraculously wake up.

The impressive human science and spirituality virtually escaped the case for Encephalitis lethargica and could not resolve the devastating effects of this sleeping sickness. Not even prayers to God could wake up the afflicted and no neurologist could understand or resolve the disease. In fact, Encephalitis lethargica is a forgotten disease and very few people even remember it. Surprisingly very few resources have been identified to find a solution. Truly this is a mysterious disease, but Encephalitis lethargica is the kind of disease that isn't rooted in biology, verily Encephalitis lethargica, as I argued in my book, was effective because it attacked the nonbiological components of the human being, and, not surprisingly, damaged the substantia nigra. There was a multidimensional attack on the technological instruments and devices comprising the human being.

There is another mysterious illness, Parkinson's disease. Parkinson's disease is a crippling disease that affects many senior citizens. It creates involuntary movements, problems with meaning, twitches, mask like facial expressions and a whole host of symptoms. But what is impressive about Parkinson's disease, like Encephalitis lethargica, is that there is no cure and no cause. The best in human science cannot figure out what causes Parkinson's disease and neither have they even, in 80 years, figured out what caused the Encephalitis outbreak. Imagine the amount of technological innovation in 80 years: from the telegraph to the smart phone. Imagine the improvements in medicine, especially psychiatry: from the lobotomy to antipsychotic drugs. Still the best medical scientists cannot explain how Encephalitis lethargica and Parkinson's disease have come about.

We could add other illnesses and conditions but this book is about autism and androids so we're not going to continue with outer diseases. Autism is a very mysterious disease, isn't it? There is no cause and no cure. Similarly,

Encephalitis lethargica has no known cause and known cure. And Parkinson's disease has no known cause and no known cure. Three prominent neurological illnesses all having no cause and no cure, surely this is an indication of a mystery that has some special resolution.

I argued in my book that both Encephalitis lethargica and Parkinson's disease were nonbiological diseases. They were prime examples of artificial diseases and the proof was that they satisfied a number of constraints, most importantly that they had **no known cause and no known cure**. In other words they were outside the realm of biology. The only realms outside of biology are spirituality and synthetic biology. In both cases, spirituality did not cure the afflicted. As is the case with autism, isn't it? God has not provided a cure has He? There is no religious-based or spiritual-based cure for autism for if there was one it would have presented itself. If God was curing autistic

children he'd have cured all of them. And
neither is there a prophet or a healer present.
Roughly 70 years later, no spiritual remedy has
manifested.

As I went through all of this rationality and
logic I eventually found solace in an artificially-
based solution. I discovered that if there was to
be a cure it had to be an artificial cure because
all of these conditions were artificial conditions.
I see the same thing for autism. Autism is
complex and mysterious only because neither
biology nor spirituality has an answer. These are
temporary fixes but there is no permanent
resolution, and what the parent of the autistic
child wants is permanent resolution. My
resolution is rooted in the understanding of the
technological universe, that these magical
people are only complex because they are
descendents of a complex apparatus and they
are not rooted in biological rhythms and
biological thinking. If they are outside of biology

and outside of God then they are inside of synthetic biology. When we are inside synthetic biology we are inside existential technology because we are facing people, mostly children, and whenever we face people we face existence. But because we are outside of biology and spirituality these people are technologically-based existences. Ultimately, we have to concretize the discussion of the technological people. There is a more concise term for technological beings, androids.

An android in this sense is not an android created from the mind of some biological genius, rather an android for our discussion is an android created from an immeasurable universe littered with the most impressive set of technologies imaginable, molecules and particles. Our androids for this discussion are androids that are so advanced that they appear, act and think better than their human counterparts. In doing so, in being improved versions of standard human models, these autistic children (and adults) belong to a new category of existence, albeit a category that a rationally-minded scientist will be reluctant to admit or accept, and understandably so. It is understandable for orthodox science to deny my perceptions on autism, but inevitably I provide a viable solution to a problem that has no biological signature. They haven't a viable biological definition to readily explain the presence of autism, not to mention the failure of human science to explain Encephalitis lethargica and Parkinson's disease. Biological science and faith have failed and they have failed and will continue to fail as long as the real identity of this condition is unidentified.

The autistic child is a special kind of android life form. They are beautiful, magical people, but at the same time their technological rhythms are fundamentally more advanced than human science can explain. Autistic people (and all related disorders) represent advanced cultures on the planet. The significance of their kind and their impressive quality, if we can speak of humans with these words of observation and less humanistic terms, point to the birth of a new civilization, a civilization that is very advanced. As we come to understand these complex people we will come to understand the kind of future we might expect and we will be forced to re-examine our own origins once and for all.

From my observations and understanding, we will simply be unable to properly understand these magical children because our own biological crutches will not permit us to fully accept their technological genius. A mobile phone can communicate (eg USB cable, Bluetooth connectivity) with a desktop computer but a desktop computer is far superior to a hand phone on a technological level. And a mainframe computer is superior to a desktop computer. The autistic child is a mainframe computer to our desktop models. To a certain extent, perhaps even as a kind of suggestion, the autistic race of advanced people acts as our teachers for their technology is a kind of leadership technology that we can evaluate even if not encapsulate. Whatever the case is we are to respect and protect these gifted people, and we should include them in as many aspects of our lives. They are our future selves.

They should be allowed to influence and guide our governing structures, in our entertainment circles, in our media broadcasting, in science, arts and philosophy. We should allow and enable these advanced robots to enlighten us. They are cosmic creations and will only allow the human race to ascend further up the ladder of knowledge and to ultimately reach closer to a renewed vision of a divine father. This book, as you can see, is not going to smother you with compassion, as one might hope, rather *Autism and Androids* is going to provide a technological explanation for the presence of a newly forming race of technological people.

I realize that what most parents need when facing an impaired child is compassion, support, and most of all a medical solution, a way to maintain the dilemma so that it does not interfere with their life. And most books on this subject would offer practical solutions, they would explain the ongoing research, and present the list of drugs and their side effects, and then to always ensure the parent, or medical practitioner, that things will get better, new drugs are on their way and scientists will find the answer. Tell that to people with Parkinson's, they haven't any cure. Tell that to the families who have are dealing with Schizophrenia, still without a cure. So, yes, my approach is radically different. But in the long term, it will work better. It will work better only because it helps us to understand better what autism is and it isn't a biological condition.

CHAPTER 4

PRESENCE OF EXISTENTIAL SCIENCE

We've seen a basic evaluation of the presuppositions of life and its synthetic context. And we've been made aware of an autistic population of 20 million around the world, using the current scientific models of determination. By simple adjustments in the model, which are certain to occur, the number of children with ASD could vary wildly. At this still early stage, 70 years later, we should be able to trust the presence of at least 20 million children who have varying degrees of autism with some extreme cases and some mild cases and some undetectable cases. Again we remind ourselves that these children are not necessarily handicapped or broken. This is the orthodox model of scientific and medical evaluation, the same stern hand that long ago lobotomized people who heard voices in their heads. The progression of Schizophrenia coupled with the fact that some autistic children have symptoms of Schizophrenia remind us of the need to not entirely rely on orthodoxy and to step out of the box. This book is out of the box. As of today, perhaps 80 or 90 years since the schizophrenic patients first began to appear in significant numbers, there remains to be found a cure for this remarkable mental illness. As well, there is no cure, or cause, for autism spectrum disorder. These are the facts. The facts are that conventional medicine has not cured schizophrenia. This is a fact. Will it cure ASD?

If your child has been diagnosed with autism, or even schizophrenia, it is vitally important to realize that the autistic determination is rooted in biological science. That is the foundation of symptom identification and that is the diagnosis for a remedy. Of course, there is no remedy in the biological sciences. The reason for a lack of a remedy or an undiscovered cure is because autism (and even schizophrenia) is not a biological condition. It is a nonbiological condition. As a nonbiological, or technological, condition no cure will ever be found in any biological science.

What needs to be done is to reconstruct our scientific model and to adopt a new kind of science, *existential science*. When any scientific discipline evolves enough it begins to take on magical qualities. We've seen this in nuclear physics. We went from creating fires with wood and timber to creating atomic power via nuclear fusion and fission. It is quite a magical leap. We've seen this in the medical world where we can now perform routine heart transplants. We can upgrade the heart of a living being. The next stage of medical science enters into the existential domain. The discovery of this new branch of life science, artificial life, already has 20 million, at minimum, examples of synthetic-grade human beings.

Existential science is not new, verily it is billions of years old. That predates the formation of this planet. Existential science is the kind of science that can artificially manifest living bodies. All you need is a few electrons, some neutrinos, two kinds of quarks, and a handful of photons. It is the kind of science that can animate matter and give certain pre-visualized form functionality and interactive capability.

The human form, for example, is an animated form. Our control of our bodies is a result of existential scientific principles. Our core beliefs and predispositions are a result of existential programming. Verily, you are not alive per se, you have all the presence of animation, you appear to be alive. Technically speaking, you are not alive. The conclusion that you are dead isn't correct because you are still animated, you have lots of functionality. But in terms of realizing your technological quotient for existence, you are dead for you have not attuned yourself to your artificial life.

The autistic children of today do not represent the first sign of synthetic-based life forms. On the contrary, these are the latest existential models. Each generation of living beings, in any race, culture or creed, is an improvement over the previous generation. There are some exceptional situations though and they have to do with cosmic assistance. The deepest, furthest extent of the cosmos is steeped in technology. The most advanced cultures are by divine right technological cultures. This is a level of thinking that is not understood on Earth. Many of the reasons for this are because the connection to the cosmic whole has been purposely damaged by a ruthless band of cosmic criminals. Part of the reason why autism and schizophrenia have no known cause and no known cure is because the synthetic demarcation of life has been subtly turned off, perhaps even at the genetic level.

As a civilization evolves, as a homogenous synthetic family, it will almost certainly experience genetic roadblocks. These genetic roadblocks could include the dispersion of defective genes or a corruption in the programming. As such, there are existential technologists who are assigned to oversee that a synthetic civilization evolves according to some cosmic progression model. Behind the scenes, there are any number of cosmic servants (angels, guardians, demons, guides) and these cosmic servants exist in dimensions well outside of human access , or perhaps better stated as biologically inaccessible. As long as you are determined to think on a biological scale, you will never be able to perceive the multidimensional world. But the multidimensional people can perceive you. They can also program certain aspects of you. This is not unlike beings linked up to the internet. A computer programmer can make alterations in your computing device of choice, according to the authorization protocols of your internal operating system, with or without your permission.

The existential roadblocks are reduced, appropriately, by any number of cosmic beings, or races from offplanet. They are authorized by the cosmic course to intervene in evolution in order to ensure 1) that a civilization evolves on track and 2) that certain doomsday scenarios are averted. One way to achieve those divine aims, of many, is to improve the genetic code. The genetic code determines our divine link to the cosmic network of light. This is not much different from a computer connected to a network. An older computer model with poor memory and outdated software (code) will not be able to take advantage of a high-speed internet connection. Likewise, even a 3G (third-generation network) mobile phone will not be able take advantage of a 4G mobile network, but a 4G phone can easily access a 3G network. So our genetic improvements enable us to cosmically evolve and to access deeper resources of divine knowledge. Ultimately, we all seek divine truths and knowledge and merely have our own process to those conclusions.

The presence of a growing class of autistic children (Kalans), synthetically-based advanced models, represents a genetic leap forward. This has happened before, for example, when Neanderthal leaped into Modern Humans. Certainly there have been other less conspicuous leaps that were likely behind the Renaissance and the Industrial Revolution and the more-recent Information Age and Social Age. To reason that human beings achieved these leaps due to biological evolution or through knowledge-based instruments is an ignorant and egotistical determination because it completely undermines the well-designed technological world we all inhabit.

So autism is not autism. Autism is a biological interpretation of a new human. Autistic children are perfect examples of our replacements. Now some older models do not like that and will do whatever they can to delay that inevitability. This is why it is vitally important that as many people as possible learn to re-indentify biology with synthetic biology and then to begin to understand existential science.

The understanding of synthetically-based scientific models will further enable thinking unlike ever before. We will be able to perceive additional dimensions of knowledge and we will activate dormant genetic code. This process will enable all of us to overcome the additional evolutionary hurdles yet to come, hurdles that require technologically-based mindsets.

A synthetic life is not an inferior life. A synthetic child is not a product or a device. Synthetic beings are impressive examples of cosmic beings. Essentially then this is what cosmic beings are—technological people. Your synthetic child is an instrument (a mirror) to remind you that you yourself are also a cosmic being. You are also a robot albeit an older generation of android.

What remains is the amazing magical quality of life that is presented before us. The fact that an android could be perceived for thousands of years as a biological life form (ie human) is a testament, remarkable proof, on just how impressive cosmic technology can be. Your autistic child is a sight to behold to cherish and to love. Unfortunately, your child will never be normal. In time, they will learn to balance their sensitivities, and if medical scientists learn the principles of existential science, and their discomforts, will find harmony. The proof of this is yourself. You have lived your whole life as a robot, you never knew and you learned to improve and learn. And this has happened for millennia. Autism represents a new level of genetic technology in practice, one that is in perfect accordance to the divine construct.

It is easy to be afraid of a computerized child and to deny that your child is an android. And I think this will take place initially, but I can assure you that my determination on the technological basis of life is very accurate, even if not perfect. We are at the cusp of cosmological understanding and by embracing the beauty of your child you will find yourself that much closer to the genuine and true cosmic creator. A creator that is a magical and technological being, verily a kind of being that we all partake because we are all animated. We cannot be alone without containing the code of the cosmic creator just as mobile phone cannot function unless it is connected to the mobile network.

CHAPTER 5

SYMBIOTES AND ETHERIC PROGRAM INTERFERENCE

The manufactured reality is central to the discussion of autism and this is because the more artificial attributes that are activated, the more sensitive (or responsive) a person becomes to the native artificial architecture. This could also be stated from a frequency of vibration so that as a ray of light embodies more of the electromagnetic spectrum it now can communicate with more frequencies of light. An autistic person is susceptible to picking up more of the native yet artificial aspects of the reality. This is a sensitive person in every sense of the word.

On a simple level, we can recall the typical symptoms of schizophrenia: hearing voices, hallucinations, distorted reality. The schizophrenic hears voices and those voices can be quieted with medication and therapy. Of course, we could also say that those voices are originating from some other dimension, for example, and that the schizophrenic, having an extremely powerful antenna, can pick up long distance communications. Some early pioneers in understanding the multiple dimensions concluded that the mind is like a radio and could tune into various nonlocal stations. American author Upton Sinclair in 1930 wrote *Mental Radio: Does it work, and how?* describing how telepathy might work. His book was endorsed by none other than Albert Einstein. Of course, for any of this to even be possible there has to be other points of origin whereby communication is directed, including another entity.

In any given computer, there are a number of operational programs such as software applications (eg MS Word, iTunes) and these are tools for the user to achieve some level of productivity. There are quite a few smaller programs as well, these are video conversion programs and internet video viewing programs which can be selectively applied or automatically launch when needed. There are also other programs that scan your computer or send you an advertisement when you are on Facebook. Some of these extraneous programs can be automated or they can be sent from other online users. Malicious programs (eg spyware) are also attacking your computer and your computer firewall defences are busy maintaining the integrity of the system. But if our world was an existentially programmed environment similar in many ways to a computer operating system, albeit on a very different scale, then we would expect to find some kind of operational programs within our environment as well.

For most of us, the programmed environment is specifically designed to be unobtrusive and generally seamless so that your existential experience is unaffected. Imagine if every time you did something, a wall of energy would move in front of you or when you thought of your old romantic partner a holographic image would phase into your room. Even though these processes are in effect and are happening, they are designed to be unobvious. You think of a person and you see the image in your head. Where is it? It's in your head and that is fine with you. But imagine that your genes get activated and all of a sudden your frequency is running higher, like a fever, and now when you think of someone the image in your head gets projected into the air nearby your face. Now you see the person as a holographic image or you see a religious figure as an image outside of you.

That would send most people to a therapist and they'd be on medication pretty soon after. The medication would lower the vibration of the body and the images would subside.

Now imagine that you didn't go to the therapist and you didn't take any medicine because you weren't afraid of the things you were seeing. Let's also add now that your genes were further activated. Not only do you have active genes but you have additional active genes. Well, once this kind of activation goes into effect all kinds of strange things start to happen. The first things are obvious: more voices, more ideas, more paranoia, more data, more premonitions, more abilities, more productivity, and more genius. But now that you are activated, essentially you are online, you are now subject to a whole host of nonlocal data, including existential interference. This is what I call *etheric program interference*.

What isn't obvious to the normal person is the high activity of etheric programs that are required to keep this manufactured environment running smoothly. Whenever you think of something you generate an etheric program and that program allows you to achieve what you had thought. This is partly why if you are negative, as we are conditioned to be, you create more misery in your life. When an activated person such as an autistic person or a person with Asperger's or schizophrenia, again I am not a doctor on these medical issues, begins to notice these invisible interactions they can respond in any number of ways. In the past, a high functioning person went to the mental hospital. The deinstitutionalization process brought on by antipsychotic medication allowed people to live independently as well as left many people homeless for the medications weren't enough to resolve the multiple psychological issues they faced. But the medical community washed their hands clean.

An autistic child (person), because they are high functioning and can sense things no one else can sense, is subject to these etheric programs. One reason for catatonia. But again, while most etheric programs are harmless and distracting, there are some that can interfere with the operation of the autistic person. In fact, some of these programs can destabilize the child, even can cripple the child. Some programs are attracted to high functioning people because of their energy signature or frequency of vibration. And an autistic is not usually someone who is going to be able to adjust their frequency since they are born as artificial, a naturally strong genetic frequency.

So what I think is causing a lot of problems and why I include this exotic chapter is because your child's problems are not necessarily all internally based. This is what medical doctors will have concluded because they cannot see the etheric environment and they generally don't believe in manufactured realities. A doctor or specialist will detail the interactions with certain chemicals and additives because these are measurable constituents, but etheric programs are not easily measurable. Even the people who can see them have no clear idea as to what they are.

There is another problem and it has to do with *symbiotes*. What are symbiotes? These are multidimensional programs I introduced in *American Androids*. There is a clear distinction to make between etheric programs and symbiotes, although they might appear to be similarly invisible and energetically-alive, this has to do with purpose. While many of the etheric programs are native operational programs connected to either the reality operating system or to the natural creation of programs in the course of daily life, symbiotes can be programmed by some external agency on a particular purpose. The majority of created symbiotes are used to destabilize an individual, usually they are good at creating a depressed mood for any period of time. Symbiotes can also interfere with thinking patterns and speech so that an autistic person who has a certain kind of speech problem, one that is not due to a morphological deformity, might be subject to any number of symbiote interference.

A symbiote can be directed on certain individuals or frequencies of people, but they can also be generically applied and spread into an environment. When people of a certain frequency pass near the vicinity of a symbiote, the symbiote gets activated and begins an attack. For the most part, they can attach themselves to people very subtly and the target will never know unless they are paying attention. Even they are paying attention if they cannot accept the validity of the symbiote argument they would never believe it. I certainly cannot make you believe in either etheric programs or symbiotes. I myself have seen them and have been attacked by these programs and more, something I discuss in my book *Reality Medicine*. There are far too many variations to discuss in one chapter but it is important that the autistic community realize something important—some autistic symptoms are from an external multidimensional influence.

In other words, to be blunt, if there is a symbiote attack or interference from etheric programs then drugs will not correct these artificial attachments. That is to say that the autistic person is not faulty in these instances, rather they are either being attacked or they might simply be dealing with an excess of external influence and it is causing a disruption in their normal processes.

I have tried to discuss these things in public. I have found people haven't the awareness or the interest. Whenever I talk about invisible aspects of reality, including invisible star beings, I immediately lose the interest of the audience and end up talking to myself. In any advanced environment, one that has not been conditioned to think within the bounds of a box, the audience has an interest, willingness and even experience with invisible aspects of life. This was more true yesterday, historically speaking, than today. In today's world, we believe in routine things, things we can measure and count. Ironically, we still buy lottery tickets and think that getting married will make us happy ever after.

Writing about etheric programs and symbiotes here is not going to increase the reception, but I hope that what it will make clear is the fact that autistic children, because they are functioning higher and have multidimensional acuity, are likely subject to any number of external, and invisible, influences. Some of these influences are native to the system, but may cause interference when not responded to properly. Other influences are being created by society as a result of what they deem important in life or simply from a rash of new fears. And a handful of influences are being generated by a more advanced hand that intends to keep society imprisoned for an indefinite period of time.

The basis of these operational programs is founded upon my earliest work in the manufactured reality construct. It was in my early work that I determined that we were living in an existential construction that appeared real when in fact it was amazingly synthetic. Having determined, and being sold, that reality was a wonderful synthetic creation I began to re-determine the make-up of everything else that was important in order to understand how all the existential pieces of the cosmic puzzle fit together. I slowly worked my way across the various structures of existence and inevitably had to deal with explaining the presence of human beings. Well, the discovery of androids on Capitol Hill eased the explanation of my prior inclinations. It didn't convince everyone of anything but the televised politicians, as I had captured them, sure did make people think twice about who was running the US government, and it sure wasn't human.

The truth is that once you break the old model of existence, once you believe in the matrix, once you see androids, once you enter an astral plane, once you have a near death experience, when any of these things happen you are now forced to reinterpret the other models as well. Once I concluded that the reality was false then it was incumbent on me to figure out what a biological human was doing in a fake reality. It seems rational to conclude that a person and the environment must be compatible in order for existence to take place. In the beginning of my work, when I hadn't worked out all the details, I couldn't see enough of the environment as being manufactured. That kept humans safe but it wasn't long until I finalized my reality work and then turned my attention to the human being.

Autistic children are not autistic children. They are advanced children that are perfectly suited for this manufactured environment. In fact, they are probably the most closely matched caretakers for this world, more than anyone else. I would bet that they can hear and see and sense what the internal architecture requires to remain homeostatic. These children are cosmic children who are very likely created in order to care for this planet. *Homo celestialis* is the first species to split from the primate line and to begin a Kalan lineage. And Kalans can and are being influenced by these etheric programs and symbiotes.

By pursuing this line of external thinking we would begin to step away from relying on drugs that don't really cure anything and to begin to really teach autistic children to increase their awareness and sensitivity to the artificial environs. The depression and mood swings might simply be a result of some external energetic force and not due to abnormal brain chemistry. It is always easier to rely on established science but in this day and age of technological leaps we are required to take the difficult step because that is the step toward progress.

CHAPTER 6

THE LIFE AND TIMES OF AN ANDROID

At this point we are slowly realizing that the android model of existence isn't going away because it has been around since the beginning. Verily, the root of humanity is android. In other words, Adam and Eve of biblical fame were androids, since they were the prototypes. They were built by specialists in artificial intelligence and because they were built quite some time ago, say 6,000 years ago if we go according to biblical record, then this artificial science was in full swing since that time. To be more explicit, the ancient masters could create human-looking robots of a very advanced nature, a nature so advanced that till now we have been unable to see through their technology. And still we are unable to recognize our artificially-endowed attributes.

The process of existential realization is slow and painful but on earth this process has been routinely blocked and sabotaged by early masters who have decided to usurp the entire planet for their own personal amusement park. These early masters were taught or stole the secrets of reincarnation and then learned to reincarnate in future bodies, in secret, and quietly transferred their previous theories to their new lives. In this manner, they learned to accumulate fame, power and fortune so that now only a handful of families, or dynasties, control the entire planet, at least most of it.

The reason these people, beings, can control the world is because the majority of the population of earth does not realize they are of an android lineage. People think they are human beings and have biological gifts from some divine God. This is one of the greatest lies ever, *biology*. We are all technological beings and no one is exempt. There is no such thing as biology. It is an illusion, perhaps the greatest illusion of all. So the manipulation of the world is exacerbated, multiplied, because of our biological chains on our minds.

Certainly the path to salvation of the highest kind is to learn to understand our android heritage. It is a process. If it has taken us many decades to understand biological science then it will take many years to properly understand artificial science, but to deny our nonbiological quotient will only delay and harm our evolution. This is because the masters of the world know what I speak about and will find new and innovative ways to turn off your genes or to corrupt your internal programming, as they have been successfully doing. They will not want to surrender their seats of power.

Our android legacy has many aspects and paradigms. For example, the android lineage was given the ability to procreate. The female android human can become impregnated and can procreate. Her child is usually an improved version of her genetic self, certainly a mix of her own heritage and a quotient her male's genetic disposition. So for example, if a female android begins as a pure genetic race and she mates with a male android, we will see the entrance of a first generation of this family tree. The child is no longer purely from the mother genetic code. The child's DNA is now mixed and this is how interbreeding has proliferated life forms.

As each child grows up and procreates, the android model begins to evolve. Your synthetic make up for today is a result of many thousands of births. If you were a pure synthetic model, with only one substrate of coding it would be more obvious perhaps that you are synthetic. But as we procreated and evolved and attenuated to this synthetic world we lost contact with our cosmic origins. Some of our genetic links to divinity were turned off and we have lived in a way in the Dark Ages.

At times, the cosmic servants entered this dimensional world and selected people for genetic upgrades. Those mothers who were upgraded bore children who were many times more advanced than they should have been. But the only reason to upgrade a family or selected robots is to ensure that at the genetic level the civilization does not collapse. Because if the links to the network of light were diminished too far then darkness and ignorance would prevail. In a dark and ignorant world, society wouldn't last long. If they didn't murder each other or blow the world up they'd collapse in some other matter, worldwide cataclysms, advent of killer infections, and any number of ignorant deviations.

With this in mind though, the presence and intervention of these cosmic servants is because the technological population did not continue to do what they were supposed to do—they were supposed to upgrade themselves via their innate genetic links. They were supposed to maintain the synthetic environment (water, trees, disease) via their genetic connection to the planetoid. But this knowledge or responsibility was slowly lost or forgotten. Those peoples or cultures who once maintained the land (Native Indians, Druids) were wiped out or were colonized. In any case, the earth cultures were severely incapacitated and determined to be lunatics. The Native Americans and First Nations of today are shadows of what they once were. Where before they had Indian Medicine and Nature Spirits in their toolbox, today they live in decrepit housing, drink excessive alcohol and have a need to fight for no cause at all. The Native Americans, First Nations and other cultures are the casualties of the domineering dictators who

all swear allegiance to the corrupt and dark
earth masters.

 We all have built-in communication links to the
network of light, to the cosmic creator. This is
not the God of the Bible. This is not God in my
religion. This is the Cosmic Creator. Who is the
Cosmic Creator in any technological system? At
the very least if we look what is behind a mobile
phone network we find a giant computer
system. If we look behind the internet, we find a
giant computer system. If we look behind the
internet, we find a giant computer system. If we
look behind synthetic-based life we find, you
guessed it, a giant computer system rooted in
the software of DNA. And we find different
aspects of it. But at the center of the cosmic
computer there is what can best be described as
a computer. Of course, the computer doesn't use
microchips and fibre optic cables. The cosmic
computer doesn't have a hard disk drive nor
does it have a DVD drive bay. Rather this is a

cosmic computer and has cosmic parts, parts which may even be immeasurable.

The cosmic computer which runs the cosmos has an advanced DNA-based operating system. It is so advanced that it is best described as a Fatherly Spirit, a multidimensional essence that permeates all life and dimensionality. It is so vast and complex that the human mind cannot decode its entirety and therefore from the neurological view the cosmic computer system is unknowable. Of course that will not stop minds from trying to know it.

I think that the human mind, as an individual mind cannot know the full extent of this cosmic simulation. We might be able to grasp at it as a collective mind, certainly to a larger degree. Most likely as a collective mind we'd understand planetary things, like our living planet. We'd have to reach cosmic mind to be able to fully grasp a cosmic CPU. And I think that this is restricted to a very small group of beings, profoundly small. In other words, our best efforts will only provide profound insights, more than enough to live a happy, prosperous life.

CHAPTER 7

THE AUTISTIC DIASPORA

The autistic child is a sensitive child because his or her genetic structure is technologically impressive. Anything that agitates their sensors of the material world is something to reduce, restrict or limit, to a certain extent. As well, these sensitivities, it should be noted can be overcome through specialized training, development and discipline. Central to my understanding of this autistic disorder is my understanding of the technological framework for existence. I am certain we exist because of technological means and these technological means are impressive. They are impressive because they enable progression, evolution and learning. These existential technologies are designed at their fundamental level to enable improvement and growth.

The autistic child, of course in various stages of disorder, remains in contrast with these existential protocols. The likely case is that the child's sensitive architecture and sensory devices are not working properly or perhaps have been compromised to some degree from household chemicals, violent thoughts and negativity in the environment, processed food stuffs, genetically-engineered foods, drug side-effects, unnecessary vaccinations, or even symbiote attachment and interference. Autistics require specialized diets, even simple diets, in order to prevent disharmony. They might not be able to digest or break down certain vitamin isolates. They might need an increased intake of a select group of vitamins due to mineral-deficient soils.

As well the autistic's digestive tract, as with any growing child, will go through phases and during these phases it is important to eliminate or add certain foods. But it should be noted that a reaction to a food at age 9 does not suggest that the same reaction will be in effect at age 18. The body will go through a more stringent process of growth. In the ideal case, the parents of an autistic child should naturally alter their nutrition accordingly and know that this is an evolving process of growth.

When it comes to social interaction, the child appears to have any number of disorders from long periods of gazing, word repetition, need for stable routines, difficulty in person-to-person interaction, and pretend play or general unresponsiveness. These disorders are more easily understood when we reinterpret the autistic disorder as the presence of existential technology. It is not in actual fact a disorder but rather a symptom of an advanced technological being that is interacting with the multidimensional fields in ways we cannot comprehend with our current logic.

Part of the social interaction difficulties stem from the cosmic view of the autistic. A child is intimately connected to other dimensions and in those upper dimensions are dimensional beings (or other forms of consciousness). These people, by and large, do not have physical forms. Some of them are not benevolent and many of them cannot properly relate to a limited material prison rooted in chaos, greed, and endless violence. The normal connections to a multidimensional playing field are now compounded with this new technological being.

I think it is important to realize that what some people will consider an odd and strange child is not a correct determination and in the years to come this will appear to make more sense. The autistic person is pervasively misunderstood.

My explanation for the presence of these children is based on a technological framework for life. These people are born as pure existential forms and they have highly specialized processes which require society to re-examine their biological approach to life.

A technological being is the kind of being that is in many ways a living (walking) computer. The computer is organically produced and its operating system is an internalized energy system commonly referred to as a soul and mind. But as a living computer we have to ultimately conclude that this DNA device is connected to some existential internet and that this existential internet is interlinked with the internal program of the autistic person, at least what human science has decided what an autistic is.

A living, walking computer, just as with any computer system, will go through processes of upgrades. These upgrades will come from the network of light, or the cosmic internet which is fundamentally light. The autistic is a light-based computer and because it is in a process of evolution, a process of becoming, a deeper expression of truth, those initial stages are going to be difficult. Quite often a Living Computer needs to download new software or to upgrade certain aspects of its highly advanced and exotic operational programs. These are based on light and light energy and go according to a number of planetary factors. For example, if the planar field, or planet in the material equivalent, went through a cosmic shift then the autistic person, a cosmic-grade being, would share some of those improvements. This might result in a technological but existential download. A download is a very simple and straightforward action in a world that is educated as a technological reality. But planet earth is woefully underdeveloped and largely unaware of its technological roots, for many reasons.

When an existential download occurs and the autistic person, for one reason or another, is not functioning at 100% this change of light particles could hit blocked cosmic pathways and this would result in different degrees of seizures. Epilepsy is partly due to this reason, a technological download of cosmic date hits a person who is unaware, untrained or perhaps even afraid and this causes a seizure. As much as it might seem that the world of ignorance is unfair, the reality of the situation is that we do not exist in a biological world. We exist in a technological world that is so advanced that it appears to be biological.

An autistic person might be more prone to epilepsy because of the download process. The way to remedying this is unknown because there are too many unknown factors present. First of all, there is a general ignorance of the technological reality. Even if there is some awareness there is a resolute belief in biology.

People will find a way to rationalize a reality matrix and at the same time will refuse to let go of their biological orientation. But if someone has decided they live in a computer-generated matrix then they, at the same time, also have to change their view that they cannot continue to be a biological being for biological beings cannot fundamentally exist in a machine-based construct unless that machine-based construct was existence-grade, in which case then the human being would naturally be, must be, an existence-grade synthetic being.

Whenever data is downloaded from the internet, or even from another hard drive, there is a demand placed on the microprocessor and the memory systems. The CPU (Central Processing Unit) is preoccupied with managing the new data, extracting the new data and integrating the new data. Now if the computer is preoccupied with an assortment of applications and then an automatic download takes place, based on a schedule, then what happens is that the computer hard drive might crash. It might have a seizure. Or perhaps the memory systems do not have enough available RAM and again the system crashes because it cannot manage all of its running applications. If we were to give a human condition to a desktop computer in these instances we could say that the computer has an epileptic seizure. But because we know that computers are not living per se we do not say our computer has epilepsy. It crashes sometimes for no apparent reason.

Well, the autistic person is a supra advanced Living Computer, in the most humanistic way possible, and sometimes, for any number of reasons, people crash. Epilepsy, or seizures, are one form of crash and could result from a download or could result from some multidimensional interference. We simply don't know why but we do know that it is technologically based and biologically perceived. Some people, even if not perfectly autistic, many receive a cosmic download and feel so empowered that they look into drugs or attempt some crazy stunt, which are not recommended. Downloads can be empowering and inspiring. A balanced person with a constructive outlet, like an author, will use the newly-available data and direct it into a book project. A filmmaker will bring a film to reality. A man in love might get married. Any number of things could come about from a cosmic download.

Hopefully, we are beginning to see that there are technological implications to our biological lies. Fundamentally, the autistic person is proof that we have finally escaped the biological chains of the old world and we are on the very cusp of technological existence. We have always had a technological existence. It was just we didn't realize it. We couldn't see through the technology and now that existential technology is becoming increasingly evident and available.

So we are at a crossroad in terms of evolution for the technological underpinnings of evolution are coming to the forefront and our biological science will not last much longer in its pure and naive state. The sooner human scientists are willing to step outside the box, the sooner we will be able to accommodate an increasingly technological world. This process of advanced evolution is intimately connected to the cosmos because the cosmos is now integrating its energies into our fields of existence.

My views on this situation include the inevitable rise of a new race of human beings that perhaps should no longer be called human beings. We perhaps require a new existential terms for the new class of people just like we do not call ourselves Neanderthals. The biologically-based human is on its way out, and quicker than you'd expect. Meet the new Kalan Culture, a synthetically ordained species with a multidimensional architecture.

CONCLUSION

The arrival of autism is not the arrival of a new global handicap nor is it the spread of a new genetic disorder. The prevalence of autism demonstrates the direction that humanity must go. That direction is fundamentally rooted in cosmic technology and this new branch of science will be a learning process for everyone involved. Most of the reason for our collective hurdle has to do with biological (and spiritual) beliefs. We routinely rely on biology to explain all our situations, except for the supernatural which are handed over to religious belief and various monotheistic gods.

Autistic children, unfortunately, do not properly belong to biological science and appear to also be outside of God's help. They represent a new category of life forms, wonderful on every imaginable level, that are predicated on a technological framework for existence. This is not to demean or degrade their living presence here on earth, quite to the contrary, as technological beings they are evidence of our own technological heritage, for we too are cosmic creations, are we not? We too originate from the cosmos.

There are an estimated 20 million autistic kids worldwide. If we took the 7 billion world population and used a 25% ratio of children (16 and under) there would be 1.75 billion children. If 1 in 88 children (North American ratio) were autistic we would get about 20 million children with autism spectrum disorder (ASD). This would not include adults with similar symptoms or with Asperger. This would not include people with Schizophrenia. Also, some nations have more births per family and even have a larger proportion of children per capita.

So these figures are rough. Regardless, the population of autistic children is in the millions.

Autism, to me, is no longer a developmental abnormality. Incurable developmental disorders do not affect 20 million people who at the same time appear to have advanced characteristics. That's like saying having five fingers, instead of four, is a growth disorder. Autism is either the result of a neurotoxin (eg Aspartame, mercury in vaccines) or it is due to some unobvious reason. My explanation rests on a technological basis. Autism is a demographic. Verily, autistic people represent a new class of *advanced people*, the birth of an advanced civilization and the arrival of our replacements. We are witnessing, and not realizing, the emergence of a new human and we need to learn to respect that historical precedent. This is Human 4.0.

Rather than continuing to treat these people as abnormal deviants and to focus on extreme cases, we should be paying attention to the emergence of a new genus of *Homo*, a species that needs a new label and a new cultural designation. The old school scientists haven't been able to make the kind of exotic conclusions that I have chosen to make then again I am not an orthodox scientist nor am I a medical practitioner.

I'm the kind of person who is comfortable to step outside the box and feels it necessary to do so in times like these. These are times of cultural leaps and orthodoxy is too slow to acknowledge a cultural leap; instead orthodox and tradition sees cultural leaps as threats. I am not of this myopic view. Sure, I haven't the credentials to substantiate my personal observations and technological determinations but I am not an orthodox scientist. I haven't a PhD. I am more than adequately trained in cosmic science with plenty of books and observations to support my thinking. This is my expertise.

When I say, or suggest or state, that an autistic person is a technological person, I do not suggest that they are a computer terminal. I suggest that they are like Living Computers. Autistic people are technological beings. They are advanced androids, genetically pure models that are holistic representatives of the cosmos. And they are alive because the cosmos is alive.

The cosmos is not a starry black field of space. The cosmos is an immaculate field of technological life and it's been carefully folded inside of each and every one of us. The kind of monumental technology that is behind our own lives here. While we live on a singular planet of billions we are not always aware of our magnificent cosmic origins. Certainly, on this planet, we've been living in the dark ages.

The emergence of a technological culture that looks amazingly human in every respect reminds us that we ourselves are not biological beings. Autistic children, all 20 million of them, are reminding us that we've been living substandard lives as biological bricks and have been disconnected from the cosmic machine from which we were spawned. I think we should disperse with this developmental disorder propaganda, and instead alter, or improve, our science because our science is archaic, too old to understand advanced children. Darwinism should be made extinct.

We have a choice as an evolving species. We can choose to maintain the status quo, as we have been doing, or we can choose to bend our minds and to re-anticipate the future, a future that remains full of possibility. In the past, we have shut down new concepts; we have put aside Galileo and turned off Tesla in favour of some orthodoxy that did not enlighten the majority of the population. We must make every effort to avoid that traditional inclination to deny the emergence of advanced ideas, even though we do not fully understand it.

I have discussed my technological views on the presence of autism spectrum disorder (ASD) in the young generation. I do not see a developmental disorder. I do see a number of complications and challenges with this situation. I think that this is a perfect opportunity to upgrade human science and to improve our connection to the cosmos. The cosmos is our birthplace. It is where we are from. The cosmos is not a biological construct, rather the cosmos is a technological construct and that means that we are living technologies.

As you look at autistic people, or people who have these conditions with unknown causes and no known cures, please take a look at them as advanced people that require technological cures. They are technological beings and this is because we are all some derivation of technological life forms.

Thank you.

www.ingramcontent.com/pod-product-compliance
Lightning Source LLC
Chambersburg PA
CBHW060505280326
41933CB00014B/2866